~~Decryption.~~

Poetry and other works by:

J.C. Collery

<u>Word Problems.</u>

When you dig for yourself you find gold not worth spending.
It's meaning to you could be more than pretending.
Believe what you see, what your mind comprehends.
It's over if you stretch your life, end over ends.

Rare like the diamond, mineral birth of an Aryan.
See life as it was, nothing close to compare,
Then,
It all became nothing,
Views life in the shadow.
No deepness allowed.
His vision is narrow.

Quote not what is right,
But is meaning to you.
This life?
Is worth giving.
My meaning,
For you.

<u>Everything.</u>

Come down off your ivory tower.
Come shit on the street with me.
I'm foul enough to know you're wrong,
With what you're telling me.

You think you know the keys to life,
And everyone should follow.
You're really just a pile of lies,
Who's words I wouldn't borrow.

It's wrong to this,
 It's wrong to that,
And now's the time to give.
A peasant has the kind of life, that I would like to live.
Free spirit doomed to walk the earth,
No care but just to give.

You talk like you have seen your life,
Beginning to the end.
I'll criticize you constantly, but I really comprehend.
That I sometimes make the same mistakes, I really can't pretend.
I just sometimes have the decency to write it with a pen.

Rubber neck.

Try not to stare, Try not to stare.
There was a sky above us, but no one seemed to care.

"You're all a bunch of slaves!'
He screamed.
The words would pierce no ears.
Remembering that question,
Sound could fall but no one hears.

I am but a rotten tree, degrading in a wood.
My views are of a different mire,
I always act as if I should.
Pardon all of my own objection,
I am purely spawn of evil.
Or am I something purely different,
My words could cause upheaval.

Life easily given,
More easily took,
You're missing like a page that was ripped out from inside a book.

I miss you.
Like a kid can only miss his father.
Who the hell am I talking to,
Why the hell do I even bother.

<u>Love.</u>

I see your smile hidden,
You keep it drowned inside a grimace.

I react a type of way,
My mind will race away from logic.

I build a tempered wall,
In only metaphor of course.

Hoping it will fall,
The slightest touch of mellow force.

This is where the story becomes
Consumed and so oppressive.
The struggle for the power excites the fire,
So get obsessive.

I feel the pressure build.
"What the hell, I never said that."
Defeat the whole damn purpose,
I say forget it and declare that.

Why do I say anything,
My opinion's never matter.
I just get stuck in limbo,
Glass houses always shatter.

<u>Full Duet.</u>

In solace,
I tip toe,
So quiet.
Words abound me.
I talk.
It rips through,
My silence,
You'll surround me.
Just listen
To the words
And see them with your eyes.
Believe
That what I say
Is truth
By no surprise.
I get a special feeling
every time we are together
I wait,
Sometimes to catch a feeling of the weather.
You warm my core just like the sun,
The warmest kind of waking.
I feel the cold
When we do part
Frostbitten,
Leave me shaking.
Despite an abstract common thought
I sit in timeless mire.
My silence sultry burns the soul
Your voice
I do admire.
Do not forget the timeless grip
That feeling will attest.
You know you can believe me,
My love will never rest.
We run away,
Two hearts intent on making such a difference.
Affect each others lives with touch
A feeling in coherence.
Two souls,
Too old,
To catch,
In mass appeal,
I flip
A mood
To check
If this is real.
It is then that I do open eyes,
The sun start gazing in.
Reflects off of your living skin
My face begins to grin.
The dreams of once such passion
Met with touch and realized splendor.
I have to sometimes pinch myself
My mind will need to render.
I thank the heavens every day
For the moment that we met,
For you're the one I've waited for,
Two hearts in full duet.

<u>Gifts.</u>

My gift to you is me…
My love is real and meaningful
Transparent as it be…
My gift to you is me.

<u>Broken Ideal.</u>

When will something come to make my effort worth the time.
Sit back and watch neglect,
Entangled souls in steep decline.
Days will always parish,
always slave to standard time.

I believe my mind is snapping, I think my age is past its prime.

I have observed the deepest agonies of self with much presumed.
I've experienced an ego death,
A testament of true.
Despair infatuated all the memories ensued.
While a darker shade of loathing for thy self is all that's due.

You can spend your whole life trying,
To fix but one mistake.
But the world may never notice
Just a tweak of your own fate.
So,
Don't ever try to be so coy or pseudo-gloom,
you'll just end up in shambles in your childhood bedroom.

And take it from a soul that's just obsessed with digging dirt.
If you mess with the wrong person you could end up getting hurt.
So let this be a demonstration of my value to you.
I could romance you with words
Imagine what my eyes could do.
I can take
Or shake a tail.
Break a move,
Or make a deal.
And I would never ever, ever lie to you.
And that's for real.

<u>Imaginary.</u>

Gallivanting,
 Through my own mind,
  All the time.
  Sick of all the feeling.
   I'm always caught up, always blind.
    Decanter full of optimistic blood,
     I'm always blue
      My lord just please don't end this yet,
       I beg and curse to you.

He sat inside a crooked thought,
With feeling all beside him.
An anthropomorphic glyph of solace,
            The suggestive thoughts inside him.
             He screamed so loud
       The echoes broke.
              And surely just returned.
              He screamed so loud that none had noticed.
         His vocal cords, they burned.
         The malice thoughts he kept inside had bent him like a stem.
The fear and constant activism had stopped him from his hymn.
                 He cried,
           "Oh please, my god, my heart could be…"
       The words that all escaped him.
             "I beg a plea, my eyes could see,
        I'm such a horrid mess,
          I beg you sweet , just have me meet
           My answer
               No more guess!"
The sky,
      It opened up to him,
            And rain began to soak him.
             The floods
      They surely filled the streets.
      His sadness only stoke him.

"Why oh why must you be so cruel!?"
As he screamed up towards the sky.
"Why oh why are you to make a fool!"
A tear fall from his eye.

The rain then stopped and sun came out,
The moisture nourished earth,
The seeds began to grow beneath,
The sun was giving birth.
"I believe I understand you now."
He murmured with a smile.
He took this feeling he felt now,
He had it all the while.

<u>Locomotion.</u>

The lead slug departs the station.
1000 tons in tow.
Countless souls flock to fill the seats.
They have come to watch the show.
Can you be humble if you know that your time is up?
Can you insist you will be loved?
Involve to answer your own reply.
Thoughts fly free just like a dove.
Exit the slug.
Rejoice the new,
Your life is still so sound.
When it is time to return you will resume.
Your thoughts are now unbound.

<u>Too close.</u>
The cold,
The ways.
They put me in a daze.
Have a lot of good times,
But also bad days.
The feeling,
I keep,
Out my chest,
My heart leaps.
Alone for so long
Just the company you keep.
Enough to end a solid plan,
Yes I'm a solid man.
Introduced to feelings that I thought were gone,
Abolished, man.
But now I wish I stayed solo,
Because a solid blow
Has devastated me one more time,
So let my feeling flow.
Like pen bleeding paper,
Not to feel another taper,
I can't believe it's falling again,
My heart is caper.
Gifted to the core
But it's nothing with out more.
So tired of being alone,
Just another day
No bore.

But apparently I'm terrible,
And so forgettable
I cant believe I'm falling for that
But that's so pitiful
So spiteful
And trifle.
Lyric's like a rifle.
Can you hear I'm writing for you?
That's my disciple.

Burning in my chest another time

I bet you love it.
I can't believe my own sometimes.
I know.
I best not covet,
Any type of feeling because I know I'll just get hurt.
I'm begging someone, please,
You make me feel lesser than dirt.

Sorry to the gills,
A silly problem.
Nothing working.
Crisis mode arrived
My saddest side has started smirking.

Just know that I'm the realest,
and
that I am genuine.
I'm over on your side
I fight the fight for you and always win.

I'm asking power please
Just be the one that's always with me
I'm tired of this shit
Just make a fist and swiftly hit me.
If it makes the feeling better,
You can do to me whatever.
I'm asking you to just trust me!

And all the better.

<u>Morning.</u>

As I lay here,
Silent.
Whispering
The truth
Under my breath.

    The fact,
    Resumes to fool myself,
    My heart beats until my death.

Ponder,
My own existence,
You will now be self aware.

    If you are not
     Empathetic
      It may rot your soul to bare.

        Sun gazing through the window,
        Pain,
        Such a melancholy feeling.

No stranger to the times of pain,
I let the feeling in.

          Just another day, no doubt
          I say
          But no words that will escape me.

    It's time to wake
    And toil in time
    The clock will always rape me.

    Don't be afraid
    It's just a sin
    To live a life of sloth.

Some are born to lay of course.
Some cut from different cloth.

No more time to think of things.
My mind as soft as tin,
I raise my head just like the sun.

It's ready to begin.

<u>Naive.</u>

Quite majestic I may say,
The sun sets over the bay.
The kids come out from inside the house to go into town and play.
I have a good riddle for you,
It sits at the bar in a brew.
You look in a glass 'till you fall on your ass and there's nothing that
no one can do.
It's all fun and games all the while,
It's worth but a joke and a smile.
The feelings exact so while it's intact.
You'll walk all alone for your mile.

<u>Festive Hell.</u>
He screams from the top,
"Why?!"
Where the answers are always so shy.
I belittle myself in purgatory trying to give you the sky.

My spirit is anguished in pain.
The type that will toll on my brain.
I sat in silence long enough,
It's time to break the chain.

Commanding myself,
I ran for the goal,
In all of a beautiful splendor.

I did not realize all of the efforts,
Would end on a negative render.

For me I can do nothing right.
Every day that I must fight.
I believe in a natural concept of life,
I hope you are seeing the light.

He sat in his progress of negation and static to find that his goals were all shot.
Rounding up courage to speak what he felt,
Then chasing it down with a shot.

The silence inside of a screaming mind,
Has no concept of worth.
This is not what the mother planned,
For this angel that she had in birth.

The gifts that I had brought to this world,
Would surely get lost in translation.
The feeling he lost in a shield of the night.
Triumph through verbal inflation.

The words?
They seem to lose the meaning
When you are accredited wrong.
I know that you may not like me,
Or even try to like this song.

The fact of the matter remains in the shadow until you are ready to speak.
It seems that I will battle myself,
8 days out of the week.

<u>Involve.</u>

You're the most beautiful thing I have
ever seen in my life.

Meeting you was the sweetest thing I have ever experienced,

You make me happy.
To love you unconditionally

for your spirit and the feel.
The most amazing tender feeling,
I always wonder if it's real.

Forever wishing
that you were always next to me,
With love always.

Your friend and lover.

Sharing special feelings.

With you and me
Under the covers.

Missing you is real.

As real as life is pain.
Don't forget how much I love you,

I won't forget about the same.

<u>Tendered.</u>

The water,
I was flailing with grace.
The shore,
A comfortable place

I wove my own way down to the shore
I questioned my worth, a continuing bore.
A tunnel shining.
A light at the end.
A familiar touch.
A beautiful friend.
The night turned to bright,
The morning began,
He sat with this woman
She sat with this man.
"I know you must go"
He said in remorse
"It pains me as well"
She said in due course.
      He sat in his spot midway up on the hill.
      Believing in her,
        She ran for the chill.
   The familiar change
   The freshness of life
            Variety is spice
           As spice is to life.
He watched and he waited
As the woman would live.
                 Her life he would cherish
                  As long as he live.

<u>Introspective.</u>

Intrepid stars.
Life,
Permanent scars.
Inception.
Occurs without the perception of mars.
Moons in Venus.
Extract life from the penis.
Inject into galaxy.
Create life,
So meaning less.
It's all a charade.
The game of life you have played.
Wrongs breed negativity.
Positively you will slave.
Every breath ever consuming what is free,
Until the soul begins it's exit to be,
open.
You're always hoping
But never see.
That it was always what you made of it,
The glory that will be.

<u>Pubescent.</u>

I'm a man.
So what is your plan?
I guess I have one.

It involves a salty tear,
Falling from an eye,
Looking down a gun.

I am sadistic.
But only half the time that I can think.
Other times, the world is too much,
So I just drink.
I only had a problem once that I could fully admit it.
So my focus became how well that I could quit it.
Then something,
Jumped into my life with no report.
I question it with everything in full retort.
Maybe that's my problem
I never stop and solve them.
I'm loved by a few,
So my beloved,
I will do.
Whatever it takes for love to get through to you.
I'm sorry
And I think you know that I do mean it.
If I could I'd get a new slate, and really clean it.

<u>Normal.</u>

When was your last hit?
The dopamine, fiend.

      Transact between bracket bars.
      Communication in between.

            The server and the user.
            The victim or abuser.

                  Left hanging on the edge
                  Your own ego, the accuser.

            Do not just be callous.
            Be heartless and obscene.

      Tear the flesh from inside,
      Hope to find a different beam.

Of light.
I just don't have the will to fight, I mean,

      I'm trying.
      I just don't think I'll slip this one so clean.

So I bite.

      Expose my own weakness to the world.
      Vulnerable, inquisitive, insensitive.

I hurl.

      So its out.
      Doesn't make a difference it would seem.
      How am I supposed to live when it always feels a dream?
      Then I wake.

            The universe,
            It slaps you like a bitch.
            Labels you, defames you, cuts you up
            You need a stitch.

      Or some help.

      But it's only you who is to fix.
      So you ponder,

Your mind?
Never ceases, always somber.
Just like all before,
in a mire your thoughts wander.

<u>Life Giver.</u>
You shiver, but are not cold.
Wise, but you're not old.
Hearts can beat forever in the mind of a shot soul.
Riddled with holes.
Like poking through a foxhole.
Life is the sniper, steady waiting for a shot, though.
Hopelessly involved in a situation so painful.
Assuming the result will bring some sort of gain, no.
Wrong.
You only stand to lose what never was.
Loss is like a knife, have you bleeding for a cause.
No gauze.
The wounds can never heal if they reopen.
Torturing myself just making sense of whats unspoken.
To you,
I just wish that you have eternal peace.
A never ending sunset on a never ending beach.

<u>Bitter.</u>

I get up every morning.
Hoping it was just a bad dream.
I awake into a nightmare.
Every day.
Stay positive, they say.
You're in a good place.
On the external.
I'm in hell.
On the internal.
Kill myself
Kill myself
Kill myself.
Hurt you,
Or kill myself.
Blood only comes when you're cut.
Pain only comes when you're hurt.
Fuck it all,
I think I am done.
Everything make sense when you taste the barrel of a gun.
Everything is fun when you're taking more than 1.
With the intent to push it past.
The white light just seems to pass,
Over her.
The heart so strong it just won't stop.
She begs us to just being her out, and pop,
A shot.
Through the heart,
To end all of the pain.
I am trying to be strong,
Not trying to complain.
But these days, I have this nagging pressure in my brain.
How the fuck am I to help her.
This is driving me insane.

<u>Listening.</u>

Yesterday, my mother asks me
"Why?!"

But I don't know.

I am sorry.
But I guess I have another reason to go slow.

"I just want to die!" She pleads.

Mother, I cannot hurt you.

She cries and stares into the ether.
Yet I still will not desert you..

By your side,
I witness, all the pain and all the sadness.
The thoughts and ideas inside my head bring me to madness.
I'm trying everything I can to hide what everybody sees.

Suicide, an option, but really only a disease.

Never.

The mother would never ever want that to be so.

The father, he took that way out so go and watch his show.
My spectacle?

Impeccable.
No metaphor,

It's real.
Symmetrical,
I try to be, to balance on this course.

Involved I choose to be for all I plan to give.
My life, forever grateful for, my Mother,
This is your kid.

<u>Cruel.</u>

Cruelty.

You're always checking in, but never here.
Expecting all the answers made for you.
It's never clear.
Remedied of ever giving notice or appeal.
You live your life with blinders, navigate with training wheels.
I'm sick of you, the most.
No desire for this discourse.
Your stupid face frustrates me,
I hope the motions run their course.
I am tired of the hatred,
I really don't do this much.
But you are an exception,
I'm rage drunk,
Kick out your crutch.
You thought that you were strong,
Independent, if you will.
But you are using me as fodder,
To pull the shots that never kill.
As I write this somber lyric,
It occurs to me no doubt,
That you're just a shitty person,

So for this reason,

I will shout.
The mountain tops,
They echo back the truths that I have told them.
I guess they are my only friends,
So with my love,
I do behold them...

Fear.

Is it a virus you fear?
The guillotine rises..
"Your words were hateful."
The Sun shines blindly.
Tremendous panic.
As the blade falls quickly,
The laws of attraction,
Have not been affected.
Infected with sorrow,
With no real surrender.
Question the madness?
A pathetic pretender.
Judge not of the man,
But judge heavy the actions.
Incompetent viewpoints,
Demand satisfaction.
In the end,
All that you have,
Is whoever will speak.
On behalf of your purpose,
No reward for the weak.
Inside is all,
But the same parallel.
The same ideas of salvation,
The same life,
living hell.

<u>Slippery.</u>
The calamity,
I call it all
Inside this dome
I fall, and fall.
My mind?
My own worst enemy.
In fact it often scares me.
I trap myself in walls of strength,
Imagined in the evenings, day,
As sun still falls,
The moon still shines,
A privilege to all that's blind.
I trap my own hermetic thought,
The symptoms seem to be distraught,
I capture what emboldened me,
and held it in captivity.
Some days a smile grace my face,
Some days I want to leave this place.
I often feel so violent,
As nature is a tyrant.
The sadness beats me to the punch,
My heart is surely someone's lunch,
As awful thoughts pollute my brain,
I feel the same old stabbing pain,
I beg and plea for something new,
While trying to impress the few,
That try to judge and perceive me,
I follow to captivity,
To find a slice of happiness.
I gloat and moan in silence,
As no-one cares to even need
The dirt to surely plant a seed.
In fact I find it motionless,
The gantry of my own success,
In ramming home my point to you,
The noble truth I find as true,
I level with the sky and sun,
Behind the barrel of this gun,
I call my words and vested course,
With little to and no remorse,

Forget all of the fortune, fame
Its not the same to need refrain
From saying what's been hurting you,
You learn to speak,
Than never do.

When every thing that drags the line,
Picks up on you, every time.
As I sit humbly toeing it,
I feel the creases, open pit
The cracks come open,
Deeper veins,
The blood pours out
The hope and shame
Compels you to forget the truth,
As all in well, and all is true
All at least for a moment, two.
Then snap back to reality,
The life I hold hostility,
To try and grasp the meaning here,
My thoughts the walls,

My prison here...

Fresh Air.

The vent.
Expecting the worse, so I repent.
A bit too early it seems so I am bent.
Very interested in you, my feelings rent.
A piece of your attention, just wanting some small retention.
Opens up my eyes, heels lighter than air they fly...

<u>Judging.</u>

Don't like what I do?
Guess what..
Not for you.
I do what I do because it helps
Try it too.
You learn very quick
Who just wants to hear.

Most sit and talk.
Mark their own points out in chalk.
Say you can take your own views

Take them out for a walk.

<u>Warm.</u>
When you're standing in the light
You will sometimes feel warm.
The glasses you wear refract light
Not pure form.

Infect,
this whole lifestyle makes the life not worth living,
That type of attention from me?
Not worth giving.

I remember the days,
So young and so shiny.
I remember the ways
Now the world just will blind me.

You open your mouth
a dull sound sneaks between.
An unfulfilled life.
An unfulfilled dream.

Don't run and don't hide.
The pride that you feel inside
Will open the gates
Grab the wheel,
You will feel the ride.

Seeds of ambiguity can only take root in immature soil.

<u>Open.</u>

Open up your heart.
My head is sore.
I'm a bore
Tear out all my love
Spike it down
To the floor
This life is relentless
It's not a joke
That's why I smoke
I seal off all the doors
Inside my house
Forever more.
Tip toe through the land mines
Inside my mind
To find a rhyme.
Regurgitate these lyrics
Into the trash
We're out of time
Photos that develop
Tell a story
Seldom said,
If my brain could control my heart
I tell you now
I would be dead.

<u>Speech.</u>

Fuck everything you know.
Not literally
It's metaphor
If I want to push a boundary
I can now say it here
Forever more
Forget yourself
You do not hold
A value
Besides knowledge
You're useless
without your speech
Your precious arts
And college.
Not free in the
Traditional
Sense of the word

Never

Not free
Not even a damn bird
Of the same feather

You're trapped
Behind a word

That you can
or cannot
say.

If this is a game,

Let me out
I will not play.

<u>Time.</u>

Another little lyric about the time that's always racing.

The world, a wheel.

I am the curb it's always casing.

Cease not to exist,
Nor wallow in the fire

This time can move around you,

Soul entangled in the mire.

Forget me not, the flower
That rises from the ashes,

As one day comes to pass,
The legacy,
it passes.

As the sun bakes down upon us,
to heat and cool earths surface

You slowly lose the fight to time
So never lose your purpose.

<u>Words.</u>
Nothing
Nowhere
Negative
Narrative.

Plush
Powerful
Promising
Positive.

Frail
Fucked
Fast
Forgive.

Love
Loss
Limit
Live.

Believe
Bestow
Beautiful
Bad

Silence
Solitude
Severance
Sad.

Malice
Meaning
Majestic
More.

Valid
Vanity
Vicious
Valor

Entrancing
Elevated
Endemic
Ensue

Glorious
Gallant
Gorgeous
Gnu

A plethora of words, with a meaning or two.

Imagine which one,

I would pick just for you.

<u>Rage.</u>

It is disgusting
The pain sparks to fire
Hold on to what was once to be
It all could be deleted.
Words mean nothing without context
I will not be defeated.

<u>lyrical poetry.</u>

Today was great.. that was until I remembered you.

Then my day was set to fire, fury to ground through...

my fist, carries a load of sepsis

so i infect the world with negativeness it's reckless.

If i spent my time in worry, sorrow would soon surround me

I learned my lesson once,
mental state far from sound see,

I've made my mistakes but never one I couldn't fix,

if love is in the world I assure it's all tricks.

another one crying about his stinkin' broken heart,

but how the hell did it get there?

some demons ripped it right apart.

<u>Nimble.</u>

Another short lived night, wake up puking with a bloody nose.
looking back i realize the real reason and it truly shows.
believe you me I've hurt like this,
                              but never hurt like this.

could you save my pain and brokenness from the presumed abyss?

I'm empty,
full of degradation denominated by a 1.
This tension in my mind couldn't be broken with a gun.
Artistically I'm following the orders directed to me from my mother.
she believes that helping you is just like helping your own brother.

Graciousness for knowledge leaves me writing you this lyric.

But my ignorance is folly, leave me screaming, you won't hear it.

<u>Concerned.</u>
Insufferable madness.
Consuming all around me.
Consuming all inside me.
Hunger hits.
Pain you shouldn't feel.
Troubles you shouldn't have.
Life you shouldn't be living.
Encompassing sun.
Another passing day.

Hours. Minutes. Seconds.
Every second closing in.
Entropy.
All things end.
My thought is over.
Back to complacency.
Fake smile hides fake feelings.
The circle continues.

Where fire breaks
through silence.
The son of morning wakes.
A tingle in a frigid spine.
Heart racing,
The chest, It quakes.
Such evil throw this soul to the fire,
The blood pumps to the surface.

<u>Expression.</u>

I was trying to think of something nice to say. but I got sidetracked,
by your eyes,
and its not a surprise that when someone loves you like I do,
there was really nothing I could do.

<u>Balance.</u>

When life hands off weight,
undivided, with structure
half witted you make a disastrous rupture.

when life sources truth
for dishonest and blame
we only fall victim to ones selfish game.

<u>Absence.</u>

My heart forever fondest has me broken.

Words.
The truest ever spoke now has me choking.
Open up my soul to see i wallow in the mire,
With this love I dance the jig within a ring of fire.
Lyric and a bit of smoke fills up my whole persona.
Chasing down these feelings with a shot and a corona.

Be real they say

The kind of words that do nothing but fuel it,
My heart and soul divided,

"I have that feeling…

..Johnny, cool it"

Feelings of universal appreciation may have brought you to my arms.

But genuine love for your soul will keep you in my heart.

Disillusioned and questioned the sweetest new feeling.

Unfamiliar attraction keeps my pulse quickly beating.

Appreciate the little things in life as you can,

Like the feeling of affection between woman and man.

Don't chase after dreams, for they need to find you.
Believe in the universe, don't be blind too.
The feeling you get when your heart matches soul
The sweetest of colors, my meaning in whole.

<u>Twisted.</u>

Here's a twist
I'll step back but only end up dissed
My mind fluctuates then my heart gets me pissed.

I've kissed,
your ass for the last time.

I'm gassed.
I've checked out, but since then I think due time has passed.

Yeah you're unique,

In my memory you often sneak,
Like a unicorn

Except it is a little ugly.
It's bleak.

I stare into the sun
blow apart my mind just like a gun
my father not apparent
you break the heart off of his son.

<u>Property.</u>

I'll use my gift.
I'll use my gift for love.
I'll use my gift for hate.
I'll use my gift to combat those,
That try to self discriminate.
I'll give my gift for peace
I'll give my gift for grace
I'll give my gift to open eyes,
That cannot see my face.
I'll tame my gift to conquer.
I'll take my gift to please.
I'll tame my gift to those that lie,
and spread the hate disease.
I'll give my gift to you.
I'll give my gift for free.
I'll give my gift if you care to learn,
I give my gift to thee.

My gift to give, you see.
My gift to you is free.
I tell this with sweet regard,
My gift to you is me.

Here is the future of mankind.

We will slowly but surely find out everything we do is inherently wrong. Making our species evolve to become the weakest link in the chain of command as far as survival. Extremely Delicate, and in superficial pain, we will navigate a world that we have created to sooth the greed we have for an "easy life." The advertisements of waste, feed our eyes their colorful and smooth images, wanting us to buy. Attending the boxes we acquire, we will commute back and forth to an otherwise unnecessary facet of our world, that ironically, we have destroyed, to create. Away from eye will be the ruins of this product. A world made toxic, and polluted by the effect of our vengeful domination of planet earth. The only joy we feel is from the short and immediate acceptance we will achieve after systems we designed show their appreciation for us. A world who "can't fix" the issue that is themself. An animal that once put things in cages puts itself into a cage once and for all. We search the universe for a place to call home but only end up more lonely and separated from our roots, and the undeniable fact that the universe no longer works for us. Being obsessed with ourselves permanently changes our ability to survive, and we ultimately parish in due order.

<u>Entrancing.</u>

I left my home hearing the plants sing.
A swift step out the door,
My leg moves, I see my pants swing.
The life that I made.
The sick trick, a game to be played,
Quickly move down the line
My skins thick, but thoughts are concave.
I fly away like a dove.
Ever fleetingly I will feel love,
But not without pain
Looking for answers, gazing sky above.
When I met you?
It was great.
I remember our first date.
Shaking myself trying to comprehend my own fate.
And what a horrid mess.
A feeling that I must be blessed,
Dressed for success, I crossed chest and then drove west.
Picked you up from the train.
The feelings that were insane
I knew we were lost
No more lost than dreading all the pain.
A vulnerable heart.
No stranger to being ripped apart.
Just another day
Going to have to play it smart.
I'll tip toe
Gently
Through flowers of entry
Searching for purpose, like a soul seeking sentry.
In other words,
I relate myself to song birds.
A beautiful gift
But only listening results in being heard.

<u>Modern Eternity.</u>

A whore for the likes,
It's all for attention.
You mention.
Your opinion on life,
My memories poor retention.
Sit back and kick up,
Brain storm,
Fills the cup.
Fluidity in mass
Just please don't give it up.
If it's hate in your heart,
I do advise,
It will part.
Positive prevails,

Evacuate like a fart.
And my favorite part?

It starts from vibration.
A few meddling tones
Like a group masturbation.

So keep on with this session,
Your moral obsession,
It's not moral impact,
More like moral infection.

<u>Bandits.</u>

This is,
the kind of stuff I get sometimes...

Others?

 It's pretty cold.
I'm not sure what is eating you,

But it's getting very old.

I shouldn't be here writing this,
Because I guess you're just too busy.

But the way you spin your god damn mood.
Love, its make me feel so dizzy.

I write this lyric to display the way,
you make me feel today.

Its sickening how much you project,
you mood into my life.
It unfair to treat me like this,
could cut the tension with a knife.

So I will wrap this silly poem,
because you say you want to read them.

But the truth is you just fuel the fire,
that makes me have to need them.

<u>Breaker.</u>

I see your smile hidden,
you keep it drowned inside a grimace.
I react a type of way,

My mind will race away from logic.

I build a tempered wall.

In only metaphor of course.
Silently hoping it will fall.

The slightest touch of mellow force,
This is where the story becomes consumed and so oppressive.

The struggle for the power excites the fire, so get obsessive

I feel the pressure build,

"What the fuck, I never said that"
Defeat the whole damn purpose

I say fuck it, and declare that.

Why do I say anything?

My opinion never matters.
I just get stuck in limbo

Have a switch inside that shatters.

<u>Decisions.</u>

My only grieving quality,
short lived and so deserving.

My callused mind will leave a whip cracked,
I'm out preserving.

I'll drink you till' I'm drunk and sick
Catch me out, I'm swerving

Ollie-Ollie-free

Show ya' face
You're not deterring.

Not me.

Not them.

Not anybody but yourself.

I'll pull you off and smell you,
then put you back upon the shelf.

*Life easily given more easily took your missing like a page that was
ripped out from inside a book.*

<u>Cracked.</u>

Forgive me

I'm not the man you fell for when you kissed.

Forgive me

I can't be happy when you are always pissed.

I'm tired.

I pull the sheets over my bashful face

I tried

To love you but you I could not solve the case.

This page is dedicated to the final lyric I was going to enlay here.
The work, was a product of intense fury and anger.
I felt it best to not add it, as it is very personal and might destroy
something that could be a help for a lot of lost souls, and with re-
spect to what someone very important to me would want.

Rest in peace, GJR.